THE MENTAL HEALTH RELIEF JOURNAL

The Mental Health Relief Journal

CREATIVE PROMPTS AND PRACTICES TO REDUCE STRESS AND PROMOTE WELLNESS

Chelsea Horton, MA, BC-DMT

No book, including this one, can ever replace the diagnostic expertise and medical advice of a physician in providing information about your health. The information contained herein is not intended to replace medical advice. You should consult with your doctor before using the information in this or any health-related book.

Copyright © 2022 by Rockridge Press

All rights reserved. No part of this publication may be reproduced, stored in a retrieval system, or transmitted in any form or by any means, electronic, mechanical, photocopying, recording, scanning, or otherwise without the prior written permission of the Publisher. Requests to the Publisher for permission should be addressed to the Permissions Department, Rockridge Press, 1955 Broadway, Suite 400, Oakland, CA 94612.

First Rockridge Press trade paperback edition 2022

Rockridge Press and the Rockridge Press logo are trademarks or registered trademarks of Callisto Media Inc. and/or its affiliates in the United States and other countries and may not be used without written permission.

For general information on our other products and services, please contact our Customer Care Department within the United States at (866) 744-2665, or outside the United States at (510) 253-0500.

Paperback ISBN: 979-8-88650-288-6

Manufactured in the United States of America

Interior and Cover Designer: Ever Pallas
Art Producer: Sue Bischofberger
Editor: Charlie Duerr
Production Editor: Ellina Litmanovich
Production Manager: David Zapanta

Cover and interior illustrations © Catherine Cordasco with the following exceptions: Shutterstock: © imagewriter: 51, © olllikeballoon: 73, © Lovely Mandala: 104; © Fotini Tikkou: 23, 77, 109, 134

10 9 8 7 6 5 4 3 2 1 0

Contents

Introduction viii

How to Use This Book ix

SECTION 1: Finding Self-Acceptance through Creativity 1

SECTION 2: The Artistry of Regulating Emotions 27

SECTION 3: Finding the Inspiration to Connect with Others 55

SECTION 4: Moving Your Body and Activating Your Mind 83

SECTION 5: Tapping into Curiosity to Be Adaptable 111

Resources 139

References 140

Introduction

Hi there! I'm so glad you found your way to this journal. I'm Chelsea Joy Horton, and I am a board-certified dance/movement therapist. I help people work through their emotions and understand themselves more deeply using creativity and movement.

I love helping people tap into creativity and movement to support their mental and emotional well-being. I believe creativity is one of the most powerful tools for growth. This was essential in my own mental health journey; using creativity has allowed me to understand myself, my emotions, and my relationships in profound ways.

I want to take *you* on the journey of using creativity to support your growth, healing, and well-being.

This book will guide you through creative prompts, exercises, and practices that will invite you to meet yourself, your emotions, and your experiences with curiosity, understanding, and compassion. This book also explores movement as a therapeutic tool, with a variety of creative activities that appeal to various interests and abilities.

As you go through your life, you are bound to experience a wide range of emotions—stress, sadness, joy, grief, excitement, frustration, and so much more. Experiencing these things is part of what it means to be alive. Being able to meet your emotions with understanding and having a wealth of creative tools so you can work *with* them (instead of against them) will allow you to navigate life with more ease and flow.

While this book is designed to support you in understanding yourself and your emotions, this is not a replacement for professional support by a medical professional. If you have ongoing or overwhelming feelings due to anxiety, trauma, or depression, or you experience persistent distressing thoughts, seeking outside professional support is advised. No one is meant to do this alone, and getting support can be life changing.

I am so excited and honored that you are here. I hope you feel a sense of hope and empowerment as you begin this journey of self-awareness and well-being.

How to Use This Book

This book is divided into five sections, each with a unique focus that will support you in creating a sense of mental and emotional wellness. Each section has a mix of affirmations, journaling prompts, practices, and exercises. The affirmations are short yet powerful phrases you can repeat to yourself. The journal prompts are written activities designed to help you reflect, increase awareness, and consider new ideas. The practices invite you off the pages of this book to explore ways of relating to yourself, your emotions, and your experiences. The exercises are activities that are done within the pages of the book that engage you in a creative process.

You can go through this book in chronological order or open it up to a section that focuses on what you need in the moment. You can also go through the prompts, practices, and exercises at your own pace, and in any order that works for you. Engage with whatever it is that you need for the day and go from there. There is also no rush to complete all of the sections; spend anywhere from ten minutes to an hour at a time. This book gives you tools and practices that you can return to again and again as you implement them in your day-to-day life.

SECTION 1

Finding Self-Acceptance through Creativity

This section focuses on self-acceptance and seeing yourself as worthy—it all starts there. If you cannot first accept yourself as you are, you will feel like you are continually fighting with yourself. You cannot criticize and judge your way into growth and well-being. Perfection is not the goal of growth. This section invites you to open yourself up to all facets of yourself and your experiences—the good stuff, the messy stuff, and everything in between. The prompts, practices, and exercises you find here will help you uncover creative ways to meet yourself with acceptance and embrace your inherent worthiness, which will allow you to approach your growth with openness and compassion, rather than self-judgment.

I am just as worthy in my flaws and imperfections as I am in my strengths.

In order to grow and heal, you must first embrace yourself exactly as you are. You are a work in progress and a work of art, simultaneously. What are the ways in which you are a work in progress and the ways in which you are a work of art?

The ability to accept yourself has a huge impact on how you feel about yourself and your life. Make a list of thoughts, emotions, and behaviors you experience when you are not accepting yourself versus when you are. See them written side by side and notice the differences.

WHAT I EXPERIENCE WHEN I AM NOT ACCEPTING MYSELF:	WHAT I EXPERIENCE WHEN I AM ACCEPTING MYSELF:

Being able to accept yourself requires you to embrace the wholeness of who you are and build a loving relationship with all parts of yourself. What are some of the parts of yourself that you have rejected? What is your current relationship with these parts?

Accepting the parts of yourself that you once criticized allows you to feel a sense of inner peace. You are no longer fighting with these parts. If you were to accept the parts that you have been criticizing, how would this change your thoughts and feelings toward yourself?

Sometimes, it can be challenging to know how to extend acceptance toward yourself. Think about a person in your life who has been accepting of you, even in your imperfections. How did they act toward you and speak to you? How did you feel about yourself when you were around that person?

It is often the hardest to practice self-acceptance when you are experiencing a difficult challenge or emotion. It's much easier to be critical toward yourself. Changing how you speak to yourself takes practice. Make a list of compassionate phrases you can practice saying to yourself when you are going through a challenging time.

Many of us learn throughout our lives that our sense of worth is earned. You may have received messages from others that you must be perfect, that who you are isn't good enough, or that your worthiness is conditional. What messages have you received about your worthiness? How did they make you feel?

Critical thoughts about yourself are simply that—thoughts. They are not truths about who you are. When you can see these as thoughts rather than unshakable truths about your identity, they lose their power over you. Write some of your critical thoughts and imagine them losing their power over you.

You were not born into this world criticizing yourself. The critical voice was picked up from others throughout your life and became the way you now speak to yourself. Take a moment to identify where these critical thoughts or beliefs about yourself originated from.

Once you recognize that your inner critic came from someone or somewhere else, you have the opportunity to rewrite these beliefs about yourself and find more self-acceptance. You get to create new beliefs that reflect and honor your worth. Write three critical beliefs and replace each with a new positive belief.

You may have learned that your imperfections are something that make you unworthy or unlovable. However, both your imperfections and your strengths are what make you *you*. How do your imperfections make you human?

When you believe that you are unworthy, you may think that you do not deserve good things in your life. When you know that you are inherently worthy, you can open yourself up to all the goodness around you. List the good things of which you are worthy.

When you are more accepting and compassionate toward your own imperfections and humanness, you can extend that acceptance and compassion to others in your life. Take a moment to feel into this compassion and write what you would say to someone who needs to know that they are worthy of acceptance.

Self-acceptance is a practice, especially when you're in the habit of judging and criticizing yourself. It may feel difficult at first, but the more you practice being accepting toward yourself, the easier it becomes. Brainstorm some ways that you can show yourself more acceptance and compassion.

You can't judge yourself into growth and well-being. Growth must start with accepting yourself as you are. Think of self-acceptance as the foundation of your growth and well-being. Now that you have been practicing self-acceptance, write five to ten ways that you want to grow in the next six months.

The Feeling of Worthiness

Imagery and body scans can be used to help you connect with what worthiness feels like in your body. Start by practicing this for three to five minutes and feel free to come back to this and try it for longer.

Take a moment to think of a color you associate with feeling worthy. Go with the first color that comes to mind. From a comfortable seated position, imagine a light of this color hovering above your head like a crown. Imagine this light descending onto your head, face, and neck. Notice how these parts of your body feel as you imagine this light of worthiness moving through you. Imagine this light traveling through your chest, arms, and torso. Notice how it feels in these parts of your body. Finally, imagine the light traveling throughout your lower body, all the way to your feet. Take a moment to breathe deeply and tune in to the feelings you notice throughout your whole body.

Embodying Self-Acceptance

This practice uses mantras paired with a simple embodiment technique to help you embody self-acceptance. Spend about three to five minutes doing this and notice how each mantra and embodiment technique feels as you do them.

Say each of the follwing mantras along with the embodiment practice:

I accept myself fully and completely.

Say this mantra aloud as you wrap your arms around yourself in a hug. Take three deep breaths. Allow these words and the hug to really sink in.

I give compassion to the parts of me that are hurting.

Say this mantra aloud as you place your hands over your heart and gently press. Take three deep breaths. Notice how this mantra feels in your body.

I am worthy of good things.

Say this mantra aloud as you open your arms slightly to each side of your body, with palms facing up. Take three deep breaths. Notice the feelings, emotions, or thoughts that come up.

Posture of Worthiness

When you begin to feel that you are worthy just as you are, you carry yourself differently. This practice invites you to imagine what it would look like and feel like to carry yourself with a sense of worthiness and self-acceptance.

This practice can be done standing or seated, whichever feels best for you. Imagine someone who feels worthy and accepts themselves fully. This could be someone you know in your life, a character in a show or movie, or someone completely imagined. How does this person breathe? How do they sit, stand, or move? Imagine the quality of their movement—is it slow and intentional, strong, light, spacious? Now take a moment to "try on" these qualities. See if you can shift your breathing first. Then try on their posture—noticing your abdomen, shoulders, neck, and head. Finally, try on the qualities of their movement. Move through the room as if you felt worthy and accepted yourself fully. Notice how this feels.

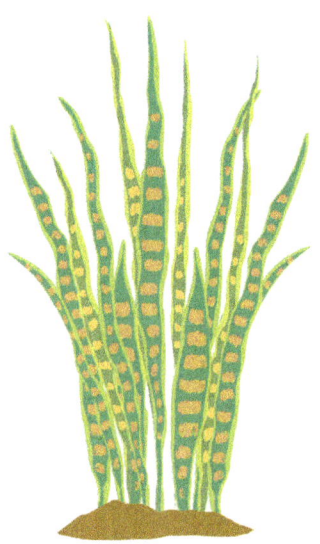

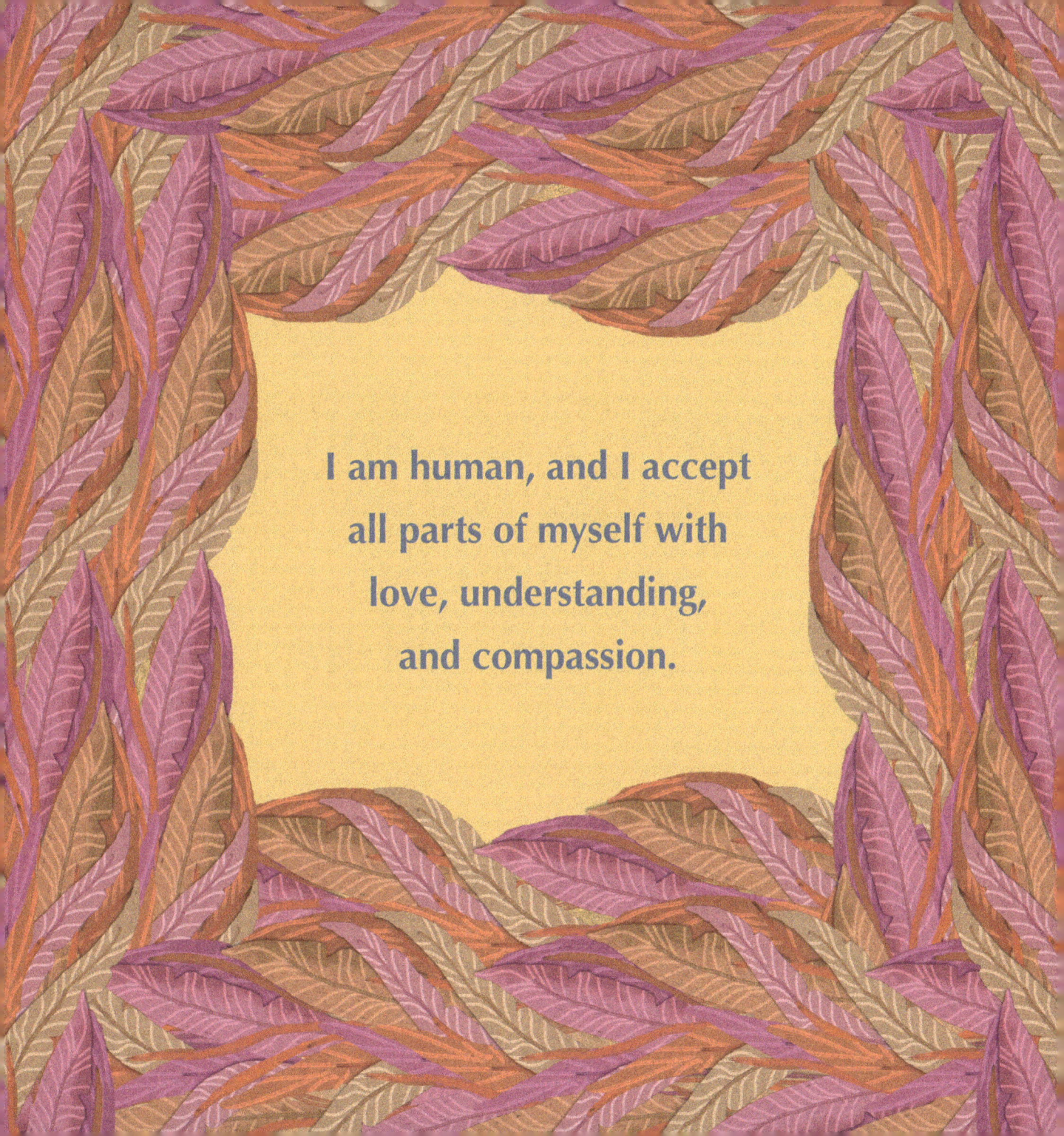

I am human, and I accept all parts of myself with love, understanding, and compassion.

Understand Your Inner Critic

This exercise will help you get to know your inner critic and understand what it's trying to do when it criticizes you. With understanding comes compassion. Fill in the blanks to identify the positive intention behind your inner critic. How does the inner critic believe it's helping you?

My inner critic often criticizes my _____.

My inner critic believes that if I am not _____ that I will be _____.

My inner critic is afraid that others might see me as _____.

My inner critic believes that I must be _____ in order to be worthy.

My inner critic fears that if it is not criticizing me, I will _____.

If this were to happen, my inner critic is afraid that I will feel _____.

My inner critic is really just trying to protect me from _____.

My inner critic learned that I must _____ in order to be safe.

I want my inner critic to know that I _____.

The Colors of Worthiness

This exercise invites you to tap into feelings of worthiness using creativity, imagery, and drawing. Draw how you feel inside and outside when you embrace all parts of yourself as worthy.

When you begin to accept all parts of yourself and know that you are worthy—imperfections and all—you feel alive, connected, and at peace. You can embrace the multi-faceted nature of your humanness. Instead of judging certain aspects of yourself as good or bad, you can simply see them as you would see different colors in a painting. They all work together to make up the whole piece of art. Use the body outline to draw the different facets of yourself and how you feel inside when you see all parts of yourself as worthy. Use different colors and images to represent the different facets of yourself. Notice what emotions and thoughts arise as you see yourself as a worthy piece of art.

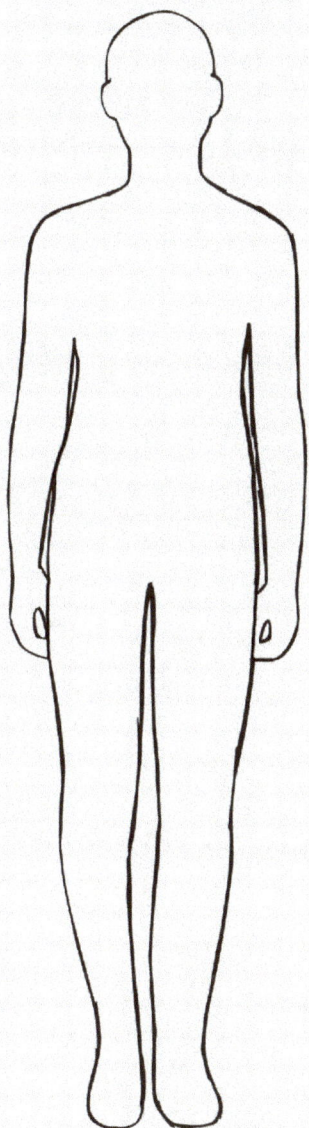

A Love Letter to Myself

This exercise lets you practice speaking to yourself with love and compassion. Fill in the blanks of the letter that follow and then read it aloud to yourself. Notice how it feels to speak to yourself in this way.

Dear _____,
       (your name)

I want to take a moment to acknowledge _____.

You've been through _____ and I know that was _____.

I want you to know that I see how _____ you are.

I truly admire how much you _____.

I absolutely love seeing you _____.

I love when you feel _____ about yourself.

I am here for you always, no matter what.

                                                   Love,
                                                   Your biggest supporter,

                                                   _____
                                                       (your name)

The Ways I'm Growing

This exercise invites you to identify the many ways in which you are growing as a person. Fill in the leaves of each branch with words that represent your growth.

As long as you are alive, you are growing in one way or another. Sometimes, that growth is small, slow, gradual, and unnoticeable to the outside world; sometimes it's significant, rapid, and hard to miss! There is no set timeline or correct pace for your growth. You grow in your own unique way, and it unfolds in the exact way it needs to. In the image of the tree you see here, each branch represents a different area of your life. Each leaf on that branch represents a way in which you are growing in that area. Write words in the leaves that identify the growth you notice in yourself.

Finding Self-Acceptance through Creativity

SECTION 2

The Artistry of Regulating Emotions

This section focuses on the importance of understanding your emotions and knowing how to navigate them when they arise, an essential key to your mental health and well-being. When you don't understand your emotions, you may fear them, judge them, or react—rather than respond—to them. This can lead to added stress in your life. You will learn to expand your perspective on your emotions with simple yet powerful tools to regulate them. Using the creative activities in this journal, you will learn how to master your emotions, rather than feeling as if they are mastering you. When you nonjudgmentally reflect on your emotional experiences and explore creative ways of working *with* them rather than against them, you can discover a sense of freedom and peace.

No emotion is wrong to feel.
I give myself permission to
feel my emotions.

Many of us learn that certain emotions are acceptable, while others are unacceptable. This creates a strained relationship with your emotions and may lead you to feeling unnecessary shame or anxiety for experiencing certain emotions. Which emotions have you learned are acceptable and which emotions are unacceptable?

....
....
....
....
....
....
....
....
....
....
....
....
....
....

If you have learned that certain emotions are unacceptable, you may find it challenging to feel these emotions. You may be placing negative meaning on them or seeing these emotions as a problem. Identify two or three emotions that you find challenging and reflect on the negative meaning you may be placing on them.

When you've learned that a certain emotion is "bad," you may find yourself judging that emotion when it arises. You may feel shame or frustration toward that emotion. In order to work with that emotion, you must repair your relationship with it. Identify a challenging emotion and write about how that emotion actually serves you.

Emotions are neither good nor bad. Think of them as simply energy in motion in your body. When you see your emotions in this way, it becomes easier to work with them. What is an emotion you are noticing in this moment? Describe how it is moving in your body.

Your mind and body are connected. Certain emotions can trigger certain thoughts. It's important to be aware of how your thoughts are influenced by your emotional state. This can be helpful when you're noticing negative thoughts. Write two or three negative thoughts you've had recently and identify what emotion may be connected to them.

Your behaviors are often a reaction to emotions. Being able to identify the emotions beneath your behavior can increase your awareness of why you do what you do. Write about a recent unexpected or undesired behavior and reflect on the emotion that may have been behind it.

When you become aware of the emotions behind your thoughts and behaviors, you can learn how to respond to these emotions in new ways—rather than reacting without self-awareness. Identify three emotions and brainstorm a list of creative ideas for how you can express or meet that emotional need.

Emotional regulation starts with being aware of the sensations that the emotion creates in your body and then learning how to shift those sensations. It's more effective to change an emotion before trying to change a thought. Recall an uncomfortable emotion you've recently experienced and describe the sensations associated with it.

Emotional expression can be broken down into three key components: how you breathe, how you sound, and how you move and hold yourself. Being aware of these components can help you have more understanding of how your emotions manifest in your body. Think of an emotion and identify how it manifests in these three ways.

Being aware of breath, sound, and movement can also help you regulate your emotions. As you change one or more of these, the emotion will shift. You can explore different ways to breathe, sound, and move to create new internal experiences. Create a list of kinesthetic things you can do to shift your emotions.

Creative expression is a powerful way to channel your emotions. Regularly engaging in creative expression gives your emotions a place to go. This allows the emotions to feel more manageable and gives you a healthy outlet. What are your favorite creative outlets, and how can you prioritize them in your life?

Your emotions want to be heard and validated. Imagine that your emotions have a voice and can express to you what they want to say. Sometimes, just being heard is enough and the emotion will pass. Identify two or three emotions and write what you imagine each would say to you.

Intense emotions can distort your perception of a situation. You might see that situation very differently when you feel calm versus when you feel emotionally charged. Take a moment to reflect on a time when you experienced an intense emotion and how this influenced your perception of a situation. How did the reality of the situation differ from your perception in the moment?

Being able to slow down and take space when experiencing an intense emotion can allow you to see and think more clearly. List ways that you can slow down and create a plan of how you will do this the next time you experience an intense emotion.

Your thoughts and emotions come and go like clouds. You are the sky—unshakable and ever present. Sometimes the clouds are big, and it's hard to see the sky, but it is still there. What are the biggest emotional clouds you are facing, and how does it feel to know that you are bigger than them?

Free Draw Your Emotions

Expressing your emotions doesn't always have to be done verbally. Art and drawing can help you channel your thoughts and feelings in a productive and creative way.

When you use creativity to express your emotions, it allows you to see them in a new light. Instead of feeling overwhelmed by your emotions, they become art. You feel a sense of control over the emotions as you step into the role of artist. Take a moment to identify three to five emotions you have experienced this week. Using a piece of paper or the space below, for each emotion, pick colors (with crayons, colored pencils, or paint) that you associate with that emotion and free draw how that emotion feels. Allow the emotion to express itself through your hand as you draw. Notice the quality of each emotion and explore translating that onto the paper. Notice how you feel as you draw each emotion.

Moving Your Emotions to Music

Music and movement help you access and connect with emotions in ways that other methods cannot. Create a playlist and explore expressing your emotions through movement.

Music connects you with the emotional center of your brain and gives you the opportunity to relate to your emotions in a creative way. When you combine music and movement as a form of expression, you can tap into your emotional core. Find a song that represents each of these emotions—sadness, happiness, anger, and peace—and create a playlist. Notice how you feel as you hear each song and allow your body to move in a way that "voices" the emotion. Notice how the music supports you as you move. Return to this practice when you need to connect with and express your emotions.

Creating Space for Your Emotions

Meditation and imagery are other effective ways to get in touch with and process emotions. Meditation can help you increase your ability to sit with uncomfortable emotions. Take the following steps to give it a try.

1. Find a comfortable seated position.
2. Take a moment to identify an uncomfortable emotion you are experiencing in this moment or one you have recently experienced. This could be sadness, frustration, anxiety, stress, or any other emotion that is uncomfortable.
3. Assign a color, image, or shape to the emotion and notice where you feel it in your body.
4. Notice if you are holding tension around this part of your body.
5. Next, notice your breath as you are also aware of this emotion.
6. Begin to deepen your breath and with each inhale, imagine you are creating space around this emotion in your body.
7. Take ten deep breaths and visualize the space being created.
8. Notice how the image of this emotion shifts as you create space around it.
9. Sit with this awareness as long as you feel necessary.
10. Revisit this practice whenever you need to process difficult or powerful emotions.

I am capable of sitting with uncomfortable emotions. I offer myself compassion as I feel them.

Emotions as Visitors

In this exercise, you will use drawing and creativity to help you see your emotions as visitors. Seeing your emotions as visitors allows you to create space for them instead of feeling overtaken by them.

Emotions are visitors. Your body is the home. No emotion is a permanent resident. When you recognize that emotions are simply passing through you, it allows you to greet them with kindness and empathy. Some visitors stay longer, and some come and go quickly. Some visitors have a lot to say and want you to listen to their stories. Some visitors simply want to be seen. For this exercise, identify three to five emotions and draw them as visitors in your home on the following page. Imagine what each emotion looks like and what they are saying and doing as they stop by. Draw elements in your home that create a safe and welcoming environment for these visitors. Notice how your relationship with these emotions shifts as you do this exercise.

Hearing Your Emotions' Needs

This exercise helps you identify what you need when you are feeling a particular emotion. Fill in the blanks to create a plan to listen to your emotions' needs.

Your emotions are often messengers, and if you slow down and listen, you may notice the need beneath them; it can be as simple as taking a deep breath or asking for a hug. A need may also require more effort, such as communicating a boundary or cutting things out of your schedule so you can rest. Being able to identify and meet the needs beneath your emotions is a valuable skill that gives you a sense of agency and empowerment, rather than feeling confused by and powerless against your emotions. You can take action in response to the emotion. Fill in the blanks below to practice identifying what you may need when you feel a particular emotion arise.

When I experience anger, I feel _____.

In these moments, I may need to _____, or give myself _____.

When I experience sadness, I feel _____.

In these moments, I may need to _____, or give myself _____.

When I experience stress, I feel _____.

In these moments, I may need to _____, or give myself _____.

Emotions as Colors

This exercise focuses on helping you shift your perspective around emotions and see them in a more positive light. You will explore connecting emotions with colors.

Emotions are neither good nor bad. They are part of the human experience. When you assign certain emotions as "bad," you may have a challenging time connecting to them or expressing them in a healthy way. Seeing your emotions in the same way you see the colors of the world around you gives you the understanding that emotions, like colors, are simply part of life—they add dimension, vibrancy, and variation. The world around us is beautiful *because* it's filled with a wide array of colors. In the color wheel here, write the emotion(s) you feel are represented by each color. Notice how this exercise changes your perspective on the emotions you have had challenges with in the past.

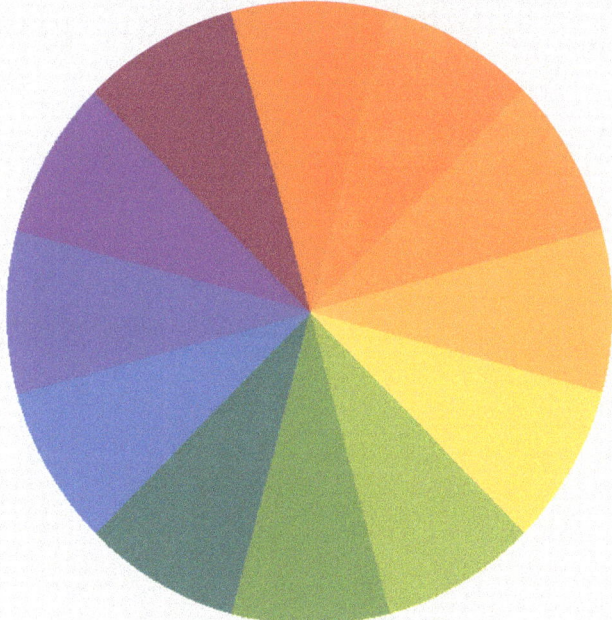

Drawing with Breath

Here, you are invited to use mindfulness, creativity, and breathing to help you self-soothe. Follow the lines with a coloring utensil and allow your breath to synchronize with the motion of your utensil.

When you've been stuck in a cycle of negative thoughts and uncomfortable emotions, it can be challenging to switch gears. Focusing on the present moment and engaging your mind in something creative gives you the opportunity to reset, step out of the cycle, and soothe yourself. Self-soothing is a helpful skill that redirects your focus to the here and now and calms your nervous system. This creates a gap or a break in the cycle of negative thoughts and stressful emotions. This exercise directs your focus to the present moment by combining breath with drawing. Pick soothing colors and follow these lines with your coloring utensil. Synchronize your breath with the motion of your hand and notice how you feel as you engage in this exercise.

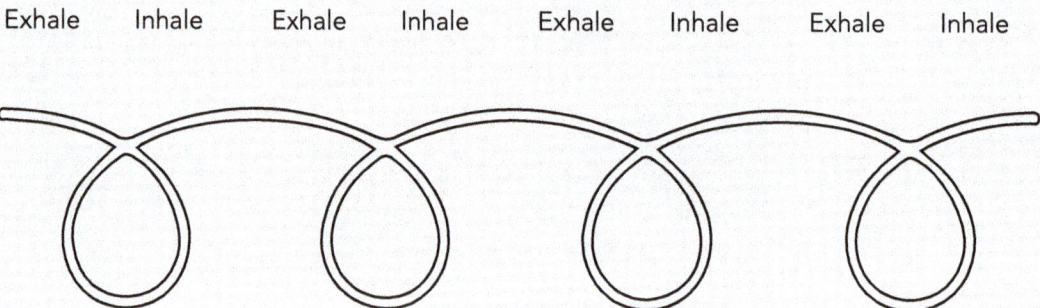

Inhale at top of the line and exhale at the dip.

Inhale at the top of each spiral ring and exhale at the bottom.

SECTION 3

Finding the Inspiration to Connect with Others

Humans are social creatures. As such, being connected to others is a key pillar of well-being. When you are connected with other people, you learn that you are not alone, and you experience deeper fulfillment in life. Healthy relationships can also help you grow in countless ways. When you don't foster and nurture the relationships in your life, you can feel isolated, detached, and more prone to anxiety, stress, and depression. Cultivating connection is a skill you can sharpen and improve, and harnessing this skill is instrumental in your journey of mental, emotional, and social well-being. In this section, you will find a variety of reflection questions, practices, and exercises to help you sharpen this skill and promote deeper connections with those around you.

I support others and others support me. I am nourished by this exchange.

Everyone has their own experiences and definitions of connection. What you value most in relationships is unique to you. Reflect on what connection means to you and write five to ten things you value most in relationships, in order of importance.

Challenges sometimes arise when you want to connect with others. It's important to acknowledge and address those before trying to improve connection. Start by freewriting about any challenges you are currently experiencing when it comes to connecting with others. This could be anything from insecurities, fears of opening up to others, or time/location barriers.

It's essential to reflect on why relationships are so important as you address your challenges with connecting. Knowing why relationships are important encourages you to continue working on relational skills, even when the difficulties may be hard to address. Write about a relationship that felt supportive when you needed it most and why the connection with this person was important.

You can't change what you aren't aware of, but once you see the challenges you have around connecting, you can come up with ways to address them. Identify three challenges you have with maintaining connections and take some time to write new and creative ways that you can navigate them.

Opening up to those in your life allows you to experience love and connection. Sometimes, it can feel difficult to make yourself vulnerable in this way. Start small. Write three to five ways that you can practice being more open with the people you trust.

When opening up to someone, it's important that you feel safe with them. This makes it easier to be honest and authentic, even if it's challenging at first. List the characteristics of a person who makes you feel safe to be yourself.

Letting others know how you feel and what you may need is an essential part of cultivating connection. Identifying and expressing how you feel takes practice. Notice how you feel in this moment and practice describing this feeling and what you might need from someone in response.

Expressing gratitude to someone in your life creates powerful connection. It lets them know how much they mean to you and creates a culture of appreciation in the relationship. List the people you are grateful for and why you are grateful for each of them.

You were never meant to go through life alone. Letting someone know when you are struggling allows you to receive support, hope, and encouragement. Write about a struggle you are currently facing and how it would feel to receive support from someone who cares about and understands you.

Sometimes, you may find it difficult to let others know what is really going on inside. You may only want to share certain things about yourself out of fear of what others may think. What are some things that you wish people knew about you, but you have been afraid to share?

....

....

....

....

....

....

....

....

....

....

....

....

....

Expressing who you are and how you feel requires vulnerability. Many people believe being vulnerable makes you weak, when, in reality, it is the most courageous thing you could ever do in relationships. Reflect on this and write about a time when you showed vulnerability in a relationship and how much courage that took for you to do.

Connection is intentional. You must cultivate and nurture the connections in your life and prioritize them. List ways you can connect with people in your life. It can be anything from a phone call to meeting for coffee. How can you prioritize these in the near future?

Both giving and receiving support are necessary for building and deepening relationships. Giving support to someone in your life can increase trust and connection in the relationship. Write about a time when you gave support to someone and how that positively impacted the relationship.

Learning to cultivate and maintain healthy relationships is a skill. When you are learning a skill, you're not going to do it perfectly right away. What matters is that you use missteps as an opportunity to learn and grow. How have your relational missteps helped you grow? What have these missteps taught you?

Relationships are ever-growing and evolving, just as you are. There may be times when you outgrow a relationship or relationship pattern because it no longer serves you. With endings always come new beginnings. What new kinds of relationships would you like to call in as you grow?

Breathing in Connection

Connection can be felt in many ways. Imagery and breath are simple yet effective ways to access feelings of connection with the world around you. Try the following exercise.

1. Find a comfortable seated position.
2. Take a moment to slow down and notice your breath. Notice your inhale and exhale.
3. As you inhale, imagine you are receiving support from the earth as you take in air.
4. As you exhale, imagine you are giving back to the earth.
5. Practice this a few times and feel the connection—the giving and the receiving.
6. Now imagine all the people on earth breathing in the same air. You are all connected by breath in this very moment. You are giving and receiving air along with every person on earth.
7. Spend a few moments breathing and recognizing the interconnectedness of all things.
8. Notice how this feels in your body.

Kindness Notes

Kindness is a powerful force that brings connection in an oftentimes disconnected world. Kindness breaks down barriers and reminds us that we are all humans who need connection. Use creativity and encouraging notes to spread kindness.

Kindness has the potential to turn someone's day around. Doing random acts of kindness not only benefits those around you, but it also makes you feel fulfilled. Think of the places you visit on a regular basis: the grocery store, gas station, work, restaurants, class, etc. Come up with three to five kind, encouraging messages or phrases. Use coloring utensils to write them on note cards or small pieces of paper, adding drawings and images if you'd like—get creative with it! Plan a day where you hand these out to random people you encounter—store clerks, servers, co-workers, friends, anyone! Notice how it feels to give kindness to others.

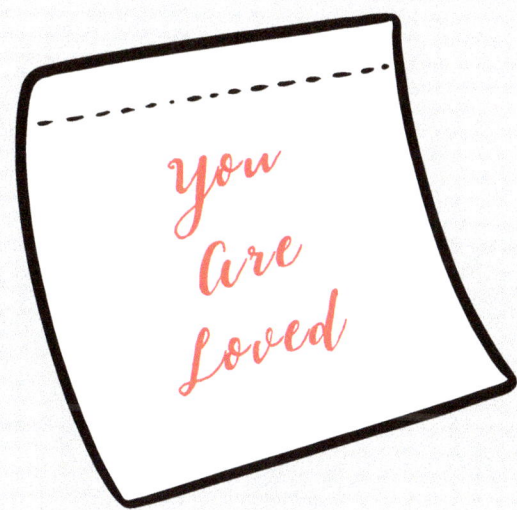

Embodying Support

Support doesn't always have to come from another person. It is something that you can do for yourself using gentle movement and embodiment practices.

1. Find a comfortable seated posture in a chair.
2. Take three deep breaths and relax into the support of the chair. Feel the support the chair is giving to your back and your bottom.
3. Allow your weight to be fully supported. Notice what it feels like for your body to receive this support.
4. Now gently wrap your arms around yourself in a hug-like motion. Explore applying different amounts of pressure to see what feels best for you.
5. Take three deep breaths as you receive this hug from yourself.
6. Allow yourself to gently sway from side to side or brush your hands up and down your arms.
7. Take a few moments practicing this movement. Notice what it feels like to embody support for yourself.

I open myself up to receive support and love. I am worthy of connection.

A Letter of Gratitude

Expressing gratitude to someone in your life is a great way to deepen connection and can facilitate rich conversation. Fill in the blanks of this gratitude letter and read it to someone you care about.

Dear _____,

I want to take the time to let you to know how much I appreciate you.

I am so grateful that you _____.

I really appreciate the way you _____.

The times that you _____ meant so much to me.

When I have felt _____, you have been there to _____.

Having you in my life makes me feel _____.

I'm so glad that we _____.

With gratitude,

_____
(your name)

The Feeling of Connection

Feeling connected allows you to feel more hopeful, optimistic, and resilient. How connected you are to those in your life has a direct impact on your emotional well-being.

When you feel isolated, you may feel hopeless or depressed. Your challenges may seem more difficult, and stressors may feel more overwhelming. Use the body outlines that follow to draw how you feel when you are isolated and how you feel when you are connected. Use different colors to represent the different emotions of each experience.

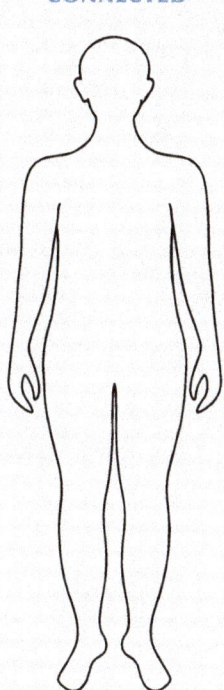

ISOLATED   CONNECTED

The Garden of Support

Support comes in many forms. You need a variety of different types of support to meet various needs. Use this imagery of a garden to identify the different elements of support currently in your life.

Just like a garden has many elements to it that make it thrive, you also need a variety of things in your life to help you feel supported. A garden has sun, soil, water, flowers, a fence or boundary, and various tools. When it comes to support, it's most beneficial to have multiple resources and relationships that you can use. It's helpful to identify all the many ways you can receive support in your life. Color the garden found here and label which elements of the garden represent the various elements of support in your life. What elements of support are foundational in your life, like the soil and the sun in a garden? What people in your life are like the water or the flowers?

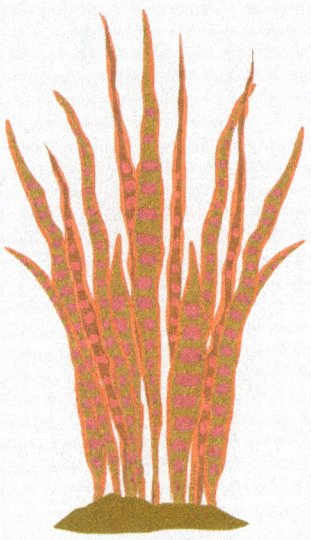

78   The Mental Health Relief Journal

The Iceberg of Vulnerability

Vulnerability means letting people see what's beneath the surface and sharing what's going on deep down. When you let someone in below the surface, this allows you to create a deeper and more authentic connection.

It can be challenging to let others know what's going on beneath the surface. You may want to share only a bit of your emotional experience, because it makes you feel vulnerable to express what you're experiencing deep down. There may be certain thoughts and emotions that feel easier than others to share. These are like the tip of an iceberg. It's what you show on the surface. The more sensitive thoughts and feelings are beneath the surface of the water and require you to go deeper. Use the iceberg drawing to identify what you show on the surface and what is deep down that feels difficult to share.

SECTION 4

Moving Your Body and Activating Your Mind

Your mind and body can be your greatest allies in creating a rich and fulfilling life when you learn how to work with them, nourish them, and use them in positive ways. You only get one body and one mind, so caring for them will benefit you immensely as you navigate the many experiences of life. When you neglect them, you may feel stressed, overwhelmed, uneasy, and disconnected from yourself. Because each part of you is connected, how you feel in your body and mind has a direct correlation with your physical, mental, and emotional health. Taking intentional care of these parts has a powerful positive impact on your life experience. Throughout this section, you will be guided through journaling prompts, exercises, and practices to support you in engaging your mind and body in healthy ways.

My body is my home.
I love and care
for my body.

It's important to create healthy habits that support your mental and physical well-being. Take time to reflect on your current habits. Write the habits that are beneficial for your mental and physical well-being as well as the habits you'd like to change or improve.

There are many ways that moving your body can improve your overall well-being. It can benefit your physical health, improve your mood, and foster self-expression. Brainstorm five to ten ways you can move your body and how each may benefit your overall wellness.

The mind is powerful. When you aren't intentional in how you engage it, the mind can slip into negative thought patterns. Using your mind in constructive ways is an important aspect of improving your mood. Make a list of positive ways to engage your mind.

The way you move your body can have a direct impact on how you think and feel. Take a moment to reflect on this and write about a time when moving your body helped improve your mood or mindset. How did you feel before and after the movement?

How you think and feel manifest in how you move your body. Emotions are expressed in how you move and hold your body and may result in tension, slumped shoulders, tight jaw, head down, rigid posture, etc. Reflect on a time when you felt down and a time when you felt positive, and describe how each experience influenced how you moved your body.

Movement can be used to support physical health, such as exercise, as well as creative self-expression, such as dance. Both are equally important in creating a healthy mind and body. List three to five ways you can use movement to promote physical health and three to five ways you can use movement for self-expression.

Stress is stored in the body. It can make you feel tense, rigid, and fatigued. Exercise is an effective way to release stress from the body and increase energy. Write about your favorite ways to exercise and how they support you in managing stress.

Exercising and staying active can be easier and more enjoyable when you do it with others. It is also a great way to improve your mood and increase your sense of being socially connected. What are some fun ways in which you can exercise and be active with people in your life?

....

....

....

....

....

....

....

....

....

....

....

....

....

Your body and mind have a brilliant way of communicating when something in your life needs care and attention. You might get sick when you've been neglecting rest. You might have negative thoughts when you haven't been caring for yourself. How do your body and mind communicate to you that something needs your attention?

Your body is incredible and does so much for you. It moves you through the world and allows you to engage with what's around you. Your body moves, feels, and breathes. Take a moment to acknowledge and list all the things your brilliant body does for you.

Your mind is powerful and does so much for you. It helps you make sense of the world and reflect on your experiences. It thinks, imagines, and creates. Take a moment to acknowledge and list the many wonderful things that your mind does for you.

Maintaining a healthy mind and body requires consistency and habit. Caring for your mind and body is a way of life. It's reflected in the small daily actions. What would an ideal day of caring for your mind and body look like? Write as many details as possible.

Being consistent in creating healthy habits for your mind and body starts with small, attainable steps, rather than sudden drastic changes. These small, consistent habits lead to more noticeable change over time. How can you begin to implement small, consistent habits in your daily life?

While caring for your body and mind requires consistency, you don't need to be perfect or rigid about it. There will be days when you forget or encounter challenges. There will be ups and downs. What are some ways you can give yourself grace when it's hard to be consistent?

Your body and mind are worthy of being cared for and supported. When they are cared for, you flourish. Knowing that your mind and body are worthy of care encourages you to keep practicing self-care, even when you don't feel like it. List the specific kind of care they each deserve.

Nature Walk

Taking a walk in nature benefits your mind and body. Use your senses as you go for a walk in nature to help you feel present, calm, and focused.

Go for a ten- to twenty-minute (or whatever length of time you prefer) walk outdoors. It doesn't have to have lots of nature to be effective. As you begin your walk, take a few moments to breathe in the fresh air. Notice how it feels just to be outside, walking and breathing. Next, notice what you see around you as you walk. Notice things close by and farther away. See the variety of colors and shapes. Then notice what you hear around you. Tune in to the sounds without judgment. Notice things you can feel to the touch, maybe the clothes on your skin or a nearby tree or plant. Next, focus on what you can smell in your environment, like nearby flowers or trees or the smell of fresh air.

The Feel-Good Playlist

Moving to music that you love is a powerful way to engage your mind and body in a positive way. Create a playlist of songs that are uplifting and practice listening, moving, or dancing to these songs.

Music has an incredible way of shifting how you feel. Your mind can become fully present as you intentionally listen to the various elements of a song, and your body can feel lighter and less tense as you move to the rhythm. Carve out some time to create a playlist titled "My Feel-Good Playlist." Add five to ten songs that help you feel hopeful, joyful, uplifted, and empowered. Put on this playlist and focus your mind fully on the rhythm, instruments, and lyrics (if any). Then allow your body to begin moving or dancing in any way in response to each song. Notice any changes in mood as you engage with the music.

I work with my body and mind, not against them. They are here for me.

Wellness Planner

Planning and scheduling time for self-care helps you stay consistent. It creates external accountability and structure. Create a wellness planner to support you in caring for your mind and body.

New habits take intention to implement! Making a plan and creating structure for how and when you will engage your body and mind sets you up for success. Using a small planner or the calendar on your phone, add two activities per week for the next month: one body activity (exercise, dance, stretching, going for a walk, playing a sport/game, or anything that gets your body moving) and one positive mind-engaging activity (meditating, reading, drawing, writing, or anything that focuses and calms your mind). If you can't stick closely to your schedule, that's okay. The goal here is not perfection; instead, start to establish your new habits and practice grace with yourself if you need to miss an activity or two.

Mindful Mandala

Coloring a mandala focuses your mind and can help you feel calm. Color in the mandala on the following page to engage your mind in the present moment.

Mandalas are geometric figures used to help you focus your attention and center your mind. Working with them can be a form of mindful meditation, as you bring your attention fully into the act of coloring. This is a simple yet effective method to engage your mind in a positive way. As you focus on the details and coloring the small shapes, you will be focused solely on what is happening in the present moment. Pick out three to five calming colors, preferably using colored pencils or gel pens. Find a quiet, comfortable space to sit down and really focus, taking lighting, sound, and environment into consideration. Begin coloring and notice how it feels to fully engage your mind in this activity.

Nature Coloring

Focusing on the beauty of nature engages your mind in a positive way and can uplift your mood. Use the scene on the next page to color and reflect on the beauty of nature.

The mind can often be noisy, busy, and cluttered. Nature reminds us to slow down and be still. Reflecting on the beauty of nature inspires creativity and puts things into perspective. It clears your mind and opens you up to the beauty of the world around you. Color in the sheet to focus your mind on the beauty of nature. Choose a wide variety of colors to work with that reflect the depth and dimension of the natural landscape. You can also play nature sounds in the background or do this coloring sheet as you sit outside to really immerse your mind in the experience.

Gratitude for Body and Mind

Your body and mind do incredible things each day. It's easy to take these things for granted, overlook them, or be critical toward your body and mind. Use this gratitude letter to acknowledge and honor all that they do for you.

Part of caring for your body and mind is recognizing how incredible they are and taking the time to thank them. Fill in the blanks below and then read this aloud to your body and mind.

Body, I want to take the time to recognize you and thank you.

I'm grateful that you allow me to taste my favorite foods, like _____.

You allow me to smell _____.

You allow me to _____ the people I love.

I'm grateful that you _____ when I feel _____.

Mind, I want to thank you for _____.

You've helped me create _____.

You allow me to _____.

I'm grateful that you allow me to reflect on _____.

Body and mind, thank you for always being there for me. I am here for you.

The Feeling of Enjoyment

You can change how you feel and improve your mood by engaging your body in something you enjoy doing. Draw what it feels like to do something you enjoy.

If your mind is filled with anxious or negative thoughts, your body may respond with tension, stress, or low energy, which creates more negative thoughts. It can feel like a vicious cycle. The most effective way to change this cycle is to shift what you're experiencing in your body. When you engage your body in activities that you enjoy doing, this can bring a noticeable shift to your mood and mindset. This can be as simple as going for a stroll in nature, playing with your pet, or dancing to your favorite song. Think of an activity you enjoy and draw how it makes you feel in your body. Use colors that represent and reflect these feelings.

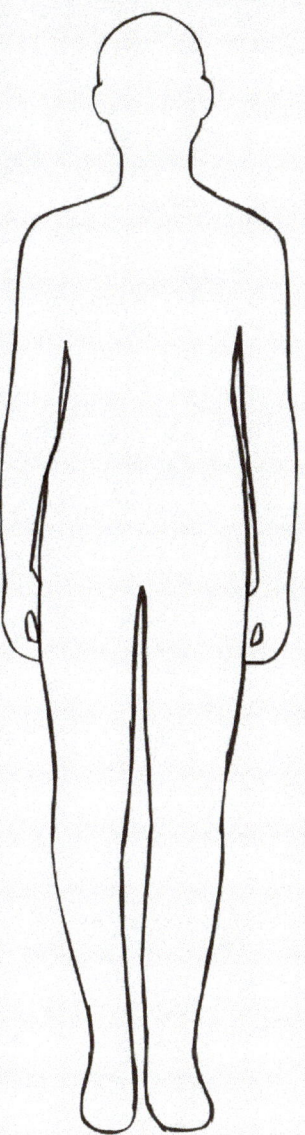

SECTION 5

Tapping into Curiosity to Be Adaptable

Curiosity is the antidote to rigid thinking and reactivity. It allows you to see your emotions and experiences in new ways so you can respond to life with mindful intention and self-awareness. Curiosity invites you to take a closer look at the things that once scared you. By approaching life with curiosity, you become adaptable, resilient, and creative in how you navigate challenges. You move through life with more trust, ease, and flow, instead of resisting change or reacting out of fear. Curiosity evokes flexibility of thinking and nuanced perspective. This section will guide you through reflection questions, practices, and exercises designed to awaken your curiosity, strengthen your creativity, and empower you to overcome challenges with more grace and confidence. You will learn how to face the uncertainties of life with an open mind—and an open heart.

Curiosity is the nonjudgmental observation of a situation, emotion, or thought. Curiosity seeks to understand and see new perspectives. Curiosity does not rush to conclusions or reactions. In what areas of your life do you see the need for more curiosity, and why?

When you approach life with curiosity, everything becomes your teacher. Every challenge contains a nugget of wisdom. You can learn from these challenges instead of believing that there must be something wrong with you for having them. Reflect on a recent challenge you experienced. What wisdom was embedded in it?

Curiosity allows you to slow down and be more mindful of your responses and behaviors. Instead of reacting from your first interpretation of an experience, you have more options for how you can respond. Write about a time when you reacted hastily and how curiosity could have shifted your response.

Life is full of uncertainty. You can't predict what will happen tomorrow. This may feel overwhelming, and you might try to seek control of the things and people around you in response. What are some ways in which you try to control things in the face of the unknown?

You can't control other people or everything that happens around you. This may seem like you have no power in your life. Your power lives in your ability to control what happens inside of you, like your behaviors and reactions. List the things you *do* have control over.

Many of us have unconscious expectations of how life *should* go. When life doesn't unfold in that way, you may feel frustrated, disappointed, or anxious. Reflect on a time when something didn't go as you expected. What were the expectations you had, and how did it feel when those expectations weren't met?

_____

_____

_____

_____

_____

_____

_____

_____

_____

_____

_____

_____

_____

_____

When things don't go the way you expect them to, it's important to honor the emotions that emerge as a result. Honoring your emotions, instead of resisting them, allows you to flow with what is unfolding. What would it look like for you to honor your emotions in the face of unmet expectations?

The brain anticipates what is to come. When you anticipate with fear, you feel anxious and worried. When you anticipate with curiosity, you feel open and exploratory. Reflect on a situation you anticipated with fear. How would you have approached the situation differently if you were curious instead of fearful?

The Greek philosopher Heraclitus said, "The only constant in life is change." Change can be challenging and many resist it. Reflect on any thoughts, emotions, and behaviors that come up for you in the face of change.

If change is part of life, resisting change means resisting the flow of life. Being adaptable and flexible in the face of change yields resilience and growth. What does it mean to you to be adaptable in the face of change?

Being adaptable means being open to the uncertainties of life. This takes incredible vulnerability. You are acknowledging that life has no guarantees yet choosing to live openheartedly anyway. What would it look like for you to live openheartedly in the face of uncertainty?

Adaptability requires you to trust in your ability to navigate challenges. Life can throw curveballs that you didn't see coming. Reflect on a time when you were faced with an unexpected challenge and how you were able to navigate it. What does this show you about your ability to navigate the unexpected?

Anxiety and worry overestimate risk and underestimate your ability to cope. This often leads to self-doubt and feelings of disempowerment. How do anxiety and worry impact your view of yourself and your ability to get through challenges?

You are more capable than you realize. You have survived every day thus far and have made it here. Take some time to reflect on how resilient you are and list examples of times when you showed resilience in the face of difficulty.

When you become curious about something, you open yourself up to seeing it in a whole new way. This can often inspire creative ideas and new possibilities for how to respond. How can you start to implement curiosity in your daily life, and how do you hope this will impact your life?

Curiosity Walk

Curiosity allows you to have a new perspective, even on things you've noticed before. When you can have a fresh perspective on something, this can help you approach your life experiences in new ways and come up with creative ideas.

1. Pick a room in your house that has minimal distractions.

2. Begin at the entrance of the room. Stand there for a moment and close your eyes. Tune in to the intention of curiosity. Feel the energy of curiosity in your body and mind.

3. Open your eyes and imagine that you are seeing this room for the very first time. Walk through the room and explore it with a curious eye.

4. Notice the shapes and colors you see. Maybe you notice something you've never really paid attention to before.

5. Become curious about any sounds you hear.

6. Experience this room that you've been in before from a new perspective. Be curious about every detail in the space around you.

7. Notice what stands out to you that you've overlooked before.

Curiosity toward Your Fears

When you are anxious about something, it's easy to want to push the anxiety away. To overcome your fears, you must become curious about them and relate to them in new ways. Creativity is a powerful way to bring curiosity to your fears.

1. Find a comfortable seated position in a quiet space.
2. Take a moment to identify a fear or worry you've been having.
3. When you bring this fear into your awareness, become curious about where you feel it in your body.
4. Now give your fear a color, image, or shape and imagine it in your body.
5. Place your hand over where you feel the fear in your body. Take a few moments to breathe slowly and deeply with your fear.
6. Imagine sending love and compassion to the fear with each breath.
7. Notice what happens to this color, image, or shape as you breathe with it.
8. Notice how you feel toward this fear as you connect with it in this way.

Curiosity, Openness, Acceptance, and Love

Life can present challenges. You might feel frustration, anger, anxiety, or resistance in response. You might even feel stuck or lost in how to approach the challenge. Tuning in to curiosity, openness, acceptance, and love will allow you to approach the challenge in a new way.

1. Find a quiet space and a comfortable seated position.

2. Close your eyes and imagine a difficult emotion, a conflict with a loved one, or any other challenge that you're experiencing.

3. Imagine that this challenge is sitting across from you. Become curious about it.

4. Try to determine what the challenge wants to express to you. Now see if you can become open to the challenge.

5. Visualize bringing an energy of acceptance to the challenge, and notice how acceptance shifts your experience of the challenge.

6. Finally, imagine what it would look and feel like to channel an energy of love toward the challenge.

7. Notice how you now feel about your relationship to this challenge. Has it changed?

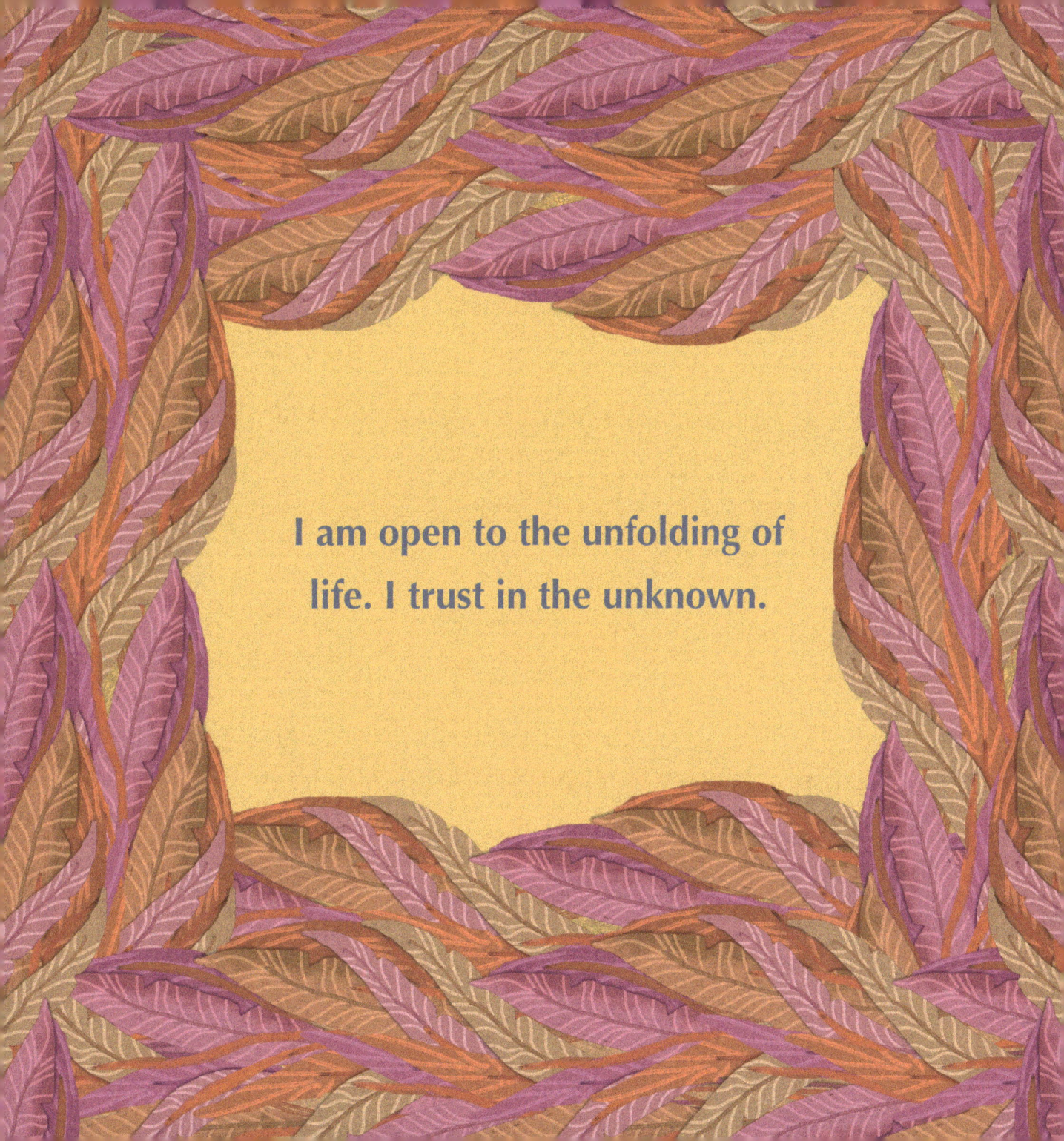

I am open to the unfolding of life. I trust in the unknown.

Flowing with Change

Think of change as the flowing current of life. Life is always moving and evolving. It is not stagnant. When you understand that this is the nature of life, you can embrace change as part of life instead of resisting it.

Take a moment to reflect on the qualities of a river. The water is always moving, flowing, and transforming. It is full of life, energy, and mobility. The water adapts to the shape of the riverbed and flows around rocks. If a leaf falls into the water, it flows with the current. Imagine that you are a leaf on the river of life, embracing the flow. Color the image of the river on the following page as you reflect on this.

The Character of Anxiety

Making your anxiety into a character allows you to externalize it and see it from a different perspective. You can use creativity to shift your understanding of your anxiety and find new ways to process it.

Take a moment to reflect on your anxiety or worry. Begin to envision your anxiety as a character or person. What would this character be wearing? What colors would it be? What kind of hair does it have? What facial expressions does it make? Allow yourself to really get creative as you envision this and use the body outline here to bring this character to life! Notice what new insights you have as you see your anxiety made into this character.

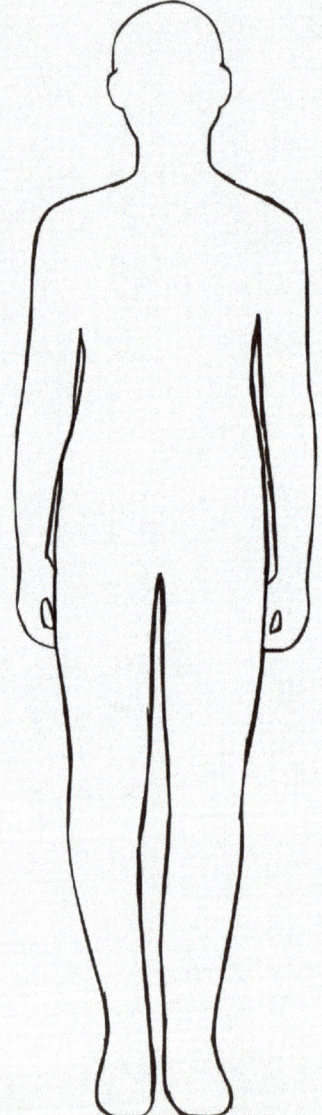

Overcoming Challenges

Knowing you are capable of overcoming challenges gives you a sense of empowerment. You can face life with confidence, rather than fearing the possibility of a challenge coming your way.

Challenges call upon your strength and your ability to creatively navigate uncharted territory. Life presents you with opportunities to step out of your comfort zone and trust yourself. It can be easy to forget how capable you are. You may have learned to doubt yourself. Sometimes, you need to remind yourself of all the ways that you can overcome challenges. In the figure that follows, fill in the bubbles by writing in the variety of ways you can navigate challenges. Examples: call a friend, express my needs, come up with new ideas, feel my emotions, learn a new perspective, give myself compassion, etc.

From Fear to Trust

The voice of fear can make you believe that you are not capable or that situations are far worse than they are. Anchoring into the voice of trust reminds you that you are capable, resilient, and supported in life.

On the left side of the table, write the thoughts that are accompanied by anxiety, fear, and worry. These thoughts might sound like "There's no way I can get through this" or "I will be a failure if I don't do this perfectly." On the right side of the table, replace each thought with a statement that is rooted in trust. This might sound like "I can navigate challenges" or "I will be okay, even if things don't work out perfectly." Notice how you feel as you anchor into the voice of trust.

FEAR SAYS . . .	TRUST SAYS . . .

Resources

Books

Brown, Brené. *The Gifts of Imperfection: Let Go of Who You Think You're Supposed to Be and Embrace Who You Are.* Center City, MN: Hazelden Publishing, 2010.

Hanson, Rick. *Hardwiring Happiness: The New Brain Science of Contentment, Calm, and Confidence.* New York: Harmony Books, 2016.

Hornthal, Erica. *Body Aware: Rediscover Your Mind-Body Connection, Stop Feeling Stuck, and Improve Your Mental Health with Simple Movement Practices.* Berkeley, CA: North Atlantic Books, 2022.

Kennedy, Russell. *Anxiety Rx: A New Prescription for Anxiety Relief from the Doctor Who Created It.* Sioux Falls, SD: Awaken Village Press, 2020.

Paul, Sheryl. *The Wisdom of Anxiety: How Worry and Intrusive Thoughts Are Gifts to Help You Heal.* Louisville, CO: Sounds True, 2019.

Podcasts

SelfHealers Soundboard

The Healing Embodied Podcast

References

ArapahoeTim. "'The Only Constant in Life Is Change.'—Heraclitus." Arapahoe Libraries. Accessed July 5, 2022. arapahoelibraries.org/blogs/post/the-only-constant-in-life-is-change-heraclitus.

Kennedy, Russell. *Anxiety Rx: A New Prescription for Anxiety Relief from the Doctor Who Created It*. Sioux Falls, SD: Awaken Village Press, 2020.

Siegel, Daniel J. *The Developing Mind: How Relationships and the Brain Interact to Shape Who We Are*. New York: Guilford Press, 2020.

van der Kolk, Bessel. *The Body Keeps the Score: Brain, Mind, and Body in the Healing of Trauma*. New York: Penguin Books, 2015.

Acknowledgments

To my clients at Healing Embodied: You teach me to be a better therapist, teacher, writer, and human every day. To my team at Healing Embodied, Sarah and Mariana: Thank you for all that you've done so I could write this book. To my husband, Matt: Thank you for loving and supporting me as I do what I love.

About the Author

Chelsea Horton lives in Southern California with her husband and two dogs. She is a board-certified dance/movement therapist and received her master's degree in dance/movement therapy and counseling from Columbia College Chicago. She has taught thousands of people around the world how to heal anxiety through the power of creativity and movement. For more about her work, visit healingembodied.com.

www.ingramcontent.com/pod-product-compliance
Lightning Source LLC
LaVergne TN
LVHW070059080426
835508LV00028B/3450